From the Frieze of the Parthenon
Acropolis Museum, Athens

THE ART OFANCIENT GREECE

by
SHIRLEY GLUBOK

Designed by Oscar Krauss

Atheneum   New York

1965

THE AUTHOR GRATEFULLY ACKNOWLEDGES THE KIND ASSISTANCE OF:
GEORGE E. MYLONAS, Chairman of the Department of Art and Archaeology,
Washington University, St. Louis, Missouri
THOMAS T. HOOPES, Curator, City Art Museum of St. Louis
MARGARET R. SCHERER, Former Research Associate,
The Metropolitan Museum of Art
ROBERTA M. PAINE, Staff Lecturer, Junior Museum,
The Metropolitan Museum of Art
ALFRED H. TAMARIN
BLAIR and JANIE AXEL

TO MY PROFESSOR
DR. GEORGE E. MYLONAS
FOR HIS INSPIRATION

Title page illustration:
Jockey
National Museum, Athens
Photograph by Alison Frantz

Greece is a beautiful land surrounded by sparkling blue seas. It has rugged mountains and valleys. The sun is warm and the light is clear. There are many small islands, which are also part of Greece.

Greek art began around 2500 B.C.

The years from about 450 B.C. until about 400 B.C. are called "The Golden Age of Greek Art."

Ancient Greek vases are the most beautiful pottery in the world. Their shapes are wonderfully rounded. Their lines are graceful. Their balance is perfect. And their decorations are magnificent. The pottery was painted with pictures about the daily lives of the people and with stories of the Greek gods and heroes.

The vases had different shapes for different uses. The slender one with the fisherman, and the one with the hunter and his dog are *lekythoi*. They were oil jugs. The large jar with the two handles is an *amphora*. It was used for storing wine or oil. Below is a *skyphos*, a drinking cup.

Skyphos
Courtesy Museum of Fine Arts, Boston

Lekythos
Courtesy Museum of Fine Arts, Boston

Amphora
The Metropolitan Museum of Art
Purchase 1947, Pulitzer Bequest

Vatican Museum
Photograph, Alinari

One of the most popular stories of all times is the story of the war between the Greeks and the Trojans. It is told in Homer's *Iliad*.

This vase painting shows Achilles, the bravest Greek hero in the *Iliad*. He is dressed as a warrior, ready for battle. He wears body armor and carries a spear.

When Achilles was a baby his mother dipped him into a magic river. The magic water protected his body from harm, except for his heel, which his mother was holding. Later Achilles was killed in the Trojan War. An arrow struck him on the heel.

The story in this vase painting is from Homer's *Odyssey*. It shows Odysseus tied to the mast of his ship so he could sail safely past the land of the Sirens and still hear their songs. The Sirens were beautiful creatures, part bird and part woman. They sang such sweet songs that sailors went searching for them blindly and crashed on the rocks. Odysseus put wax into the ears of his sailors so they could not hear the Sirens' music.

This vase was painted black; but the figures were left unpainted, except for a few little lines. The figures kept the natural color of the clay. This is called a *red-figured vase*.

Olive trees grow well in the warm sunshine of Greece. In ancient times olive oil was very important in the lives of the people. It was used for food. It was burned in lamps. And athletes rubbed it on their bodies.

This is an *amphora*, probably used for storing olive oil. It is decorated with a picture of an olive harvest.

The background of this jar was left in the natural color of the clay. The figures were painted black. This is called a *black-figured vase*.

This vase painting is a school scene. It shows how boys of ancient Greece were taught music and poetry. One student is playing the lyre with his teacher. The lyre is an ancient musical instrument.

Another student stands before his reading teacher. The teacher is holding a long roll of papyrus with Greek writing. The boy is reciting a poem. The man with a cane is the boy's servant, who brought him to school.

Greek boys started school when they were six years old. They learned reading, writing, arithmetic, music, athletics, and stories of the Greek heroes.

The vase above shows men weighing grain. A man is bending over to put it on one of the pans of a scale. Two other men hold the scale steady.

At the right is a vase painting showing a scene from a play. The ancient Greeks loved the theatre. Their plays are famous. They were put on in daylight, in big, open-air theatres. Some of the plays were serious and some were funny. All of the actors were men. They wore masks.

This painting has all the fun of a comedy.

National
Museum, Athens
Photograph
by Nellys

The Greeks believed in many gods. Some of them lived on Mount Olympus. The gods were thought to take part in the lives of the people. Zeus was king of the gods. He ruled the heavens and the earth. He threw thunderbolts, to make lightning. The wonderful head of Zeus, on the left, is part of one of the finest original Greek bronze statues ever found. The head is strong and powerful. The statue was found in the sea. Some scholars think it may be Poseidon, brother of Zeus and ruler of the sea.

Below is a marble statue of Hermes, the messenger of the gods. He is carrying his infant brother, the god Dionysus. Most marble statues from ancient times have been lost or broken. This is the only statue we have today by a well-known ancient Greek artist. The artist was Praxiteles. Another well known artist, named Polykleitos, wrote a book called *The Canon*, which means *rule*. It told how to make a perfect statue.

Olympia Museum
Photograph, Alinari

We know about many lost Greek statues from Roman copies. This marble statue of Aphrodite, goddess of love, is known as the "Venus de Milo."

Aphrodite stands with her body slightly twisted and one shoulder raised. The curved pose makes her look graceful. She seems ready to move.

The statue was made in two parts. They were joined together where the drapery begins. The arms were lost and have never been found.

The Greeks tried to make their statues look like perfect people. They tried to make them as beautiful as beautiful can be.

Louvre, Paris
Photograph, Alinari

14

Apollo was the god of light. He was also the god of music, medicine and archery.

This marble Apollo was made about two hundred and fifty years before "Venus de Milo," when Greek art was stiff.

The statue was part of a decoration on The Temple of Zeus at Olympia. A group of figures is in fierce battle. Apollo stands calmly in the center of the group, making the right side win.

Apollo always looks young. He was the most handsome of the Greek gods. Even today people call a very handsome man "an Apollo."

This magnificent marble temple was built for Athena Parthenos, the patron goddess of the city of Athens. It is called the *Parthenon*. It stands on the Acropolis, a flat-topped hill overlooking Athens.

The Parthenon is said to be the most beautiful building ever built. Every line of the temple looks straight. But really, every line has a slight curve that is difficult to notice. The stones were fitted together so carefully that it was hard to find the cracks between them.

The Parthenon was built in the Golden Age of Greek Art. It was begun in 447 B.C. and finished fifteen years later.

Pheidias, one of the greatest artists of ancient Greece, designed the sculpture for the Parthenon.

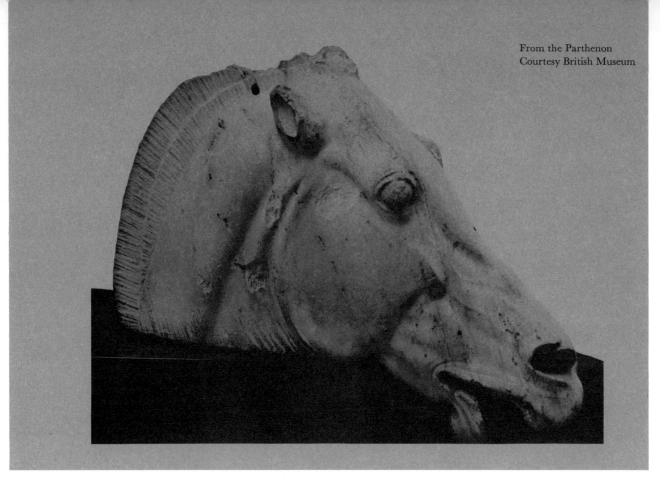

The triangular space made by the peak of a roof and the slope of its sides is called a *pediment*. The corners of the east pediment of the Parthenon had marble carvings of the horses of the sun and the moon.

This is the head of a horse of the moon. It seems worn out from pulling the moon chariot all night. Its eyes look tired and its mouth droops. It is sinking below the horizon after racing through the sky until dawn.

On the right is a marble statue of the goddess Athena. The sculptor who made this Athena wanted her to look more beautiful than any real person. Her nose starts higher than most human noses. It starts at her forehead. Her hair seems soft and curly against the flat headband. This Athena is gentle and thoughtful.

Museum Civico, Bologna, Photograph by Clarence Kennedy

This is a statue of Pericles.
He was the most famous leader
of the ancient Greeks. He was
the leader of Athens when the
Parthenon was built.
"The Golden Age"
is also called
"The Age of Pericles."

Every four years the people of Athens held a parade to honor Athena Parthenos, and to bring a new robe to her statue on the Acropolis. The parade is shown on a frieze on the outside face of the walls of the *cella*, or temple proper, of the Parthenon. The frieze is a broad band of sculpture above the height of the columns.

The figures are the gods Poseidon, Apollo, and the goddess Artemis, in the Parthenon frieze, waiting for the parade to arrive on the Acropolis. The procession, or parade, is made up of about six hundred lifelike figures.

Acropolis Museum, Athens

At the left is a gold armlet decorated with a figure of a Triton holding a small Eros, or Cupid. A Triton is a strange creature of Greek mythology, half man and half fish.

Above is an unusual golden earring. It is two inches high. It shows Nike, the winged goddess of Victory, driving her chariot through the sky. The earring is beautifully

made. It is full of action. Nike bends forward holding the tiny reins. The horses prance. The earring was probably made to be worn as an ornament by the statue of a goddess.

Even Greek money was beautiful. The fine pictures on the coins show where they were made. The most important coins in the ancient world were known as "The Owls of Athens."

At the right is a silver ornament for a necklace. The figure is half goat and half man. His name is Pan. He was a gay god who loved music and fun.

The Metropolitan Museum of Art
Rogers Fund, 1922

Warriors were favorite subjects of Greek art. This is a small bronze statue of an ancient Greek foot soldier. Greek men were proud of their bravery in battle. They were also proud to be citizens of their cities and to help make their own laws.

The warrior is fully armed with a helmet, breastplate and greaves. The greaves protect his legs. He carries a round shield. Some parts of his body are without armor so that he can move swiftly in battle. He is ready to throw a weapon, probably a spear.

His helmet covers his whole head, but there is an opening for his eyes and mouth. The nose piece comes down from the forehead.

This wonderful helmet is in the shape of a ram's head. Even the cheek pieces, which fit over the sides of the face, are shaped like rams' heads. The main part was hammered out of a single sheet of bronze, except for the horns and ears. They were put on separately. The eyes are ivory.

The crest is shaped like a horse's tail. It is made of silver.

The original bronze of the helmet was found in good condition. The nosepiece, horns and eyes had to be replaced. The crest was broken and had to be remade.

The design of the helmet is beautiful. It is richly decorated. The helmet must have been for special occasions, such as parades.

Helmet After Restoration
Courtesy City Art Museum of St. Louis

Myths are stories of gods and heroes, who did strange and wonderful things. Greek myths are still read and loved today.

One of the great heroes of Greek myths was Herakles, who is better known as Hercules. This marble head of Herakles is remarkable for the way that his thick hair and heavy beard are carved. Heavy hair and beards were signs of strength.

At the right, is a statue of Herakles as a young fighter. He is kneeling on one knee, looking straight ahead at his target and taking aim, ready to shoot an arrow. The statue is beautifully balanced by the straight body and the outstretched arms and leg. Herakles wears a helmet made of a lion's head. One of the very brave things he did was to kill a lion with his bare hands.

The Metropolitan Museum of Art
Photograph by Alfred H. Tamarin
Fletcher Fund, 1927

Glyptothek Munich   Photograph, Bruckmann

27

The Metropolitan Museum of Art
Rogers Fund, 1921

Courtesy Walters Art Gallery, Baltimore

Courtesy Museum of Fine Arts, Boston

The bronze figure at the top was made more than 2,700 years ago. It is a strong figure of a horse standing still. Powerful curves and shapes show its ears, mane, tail and legs. Yet it does not look like a real horse. It only gives the feeling of a horse.

The amusing lion and the man on horseback were made two hundred years later. They are in motion. They look like real animals and a real person.

This strange and bird-like creature is a griffin. A griffin had a lion's body and a bird's head. This one looks fierce. His mouth is open and his tongue is out.

He stretches his neck and perks up his ears, ready for action.

This was a decoration on a cauldron. A cauldron is a large metal pot for boiling water. The griffin was a favorite form of decoration in Greek art.

The statuette on the left was moulded out of clay and baked. Baked clay is called *terra cotta*.

The object is little, yet there is power in the two brave warriors riding the chariot drawn by four lively horses. The figures are simple. There is no decoration or detail.

The figure of the man on horseback, below, has much more detail. This shows that it was made later. It is also of clay. It is moulded only on one side. The back of the figure is flat and smooth.

The subject is the young hero, Bellerophon, riding the winged horse, Pegasus. He is fighting the Chimaera, a fire-breathing monster, part dragon, part lion and part goat.

Courtesy Museum of Fine Arts, Boston

Courtesy City Art Museum of St. Louis

The little terra cotta figure with the flat head and the pinched-in nose looks like a bird. Her eyes are two large dots. Her arms are like out-spread wings. She is from Mycenae, in southern Greece. She was made three thousand years ago. The striped bull, below, is from Mycenae, too. It is only three and a half inches tall and looks like a toy. The ape riding the merry donkey, above, also looks like a plaything.

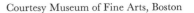

Courtesy City Art Museum of St.

Courtesy Museum of Fine Arts, Boston

Courtesy Museum of Fine Arts, Boston

The small terra cotta statue on the right may have been a doll. The body is shaped like a bell. It is gaily painted with birds and decorated with other interesting shapes. It has a long neck and round, staring eyes. The body was made in the same way as a vase. The legs, neck and head were attached later.

Above is a gentle figure of a mother goose, taking care of her three goslings.

33

Artists showed athletes in many different sports. This is a bronze statue of a professional boxer, who may have just lost a match. He is tired. His muscles sag. This statue was made after Rome conquered Greece. It is very lifelike.

The discus thrower on the right is a marble copy of an ancient bronze statue by Myron. The original statue is lost. The athlete is about ready to throw the round discus. His body is in perfect balance, as if ready to swing into action.

Terme Museum, Rome
Photograph, Anderson

Terme Museum, Rome
Photograph, Alinari

Chariot racing was a very popular sport in ancient Greece. This proud bronze charioteer once stood near the Temple of Apollo at Delphi. He was in a chariot, holding the reins of four bronze horses.

The charioteer's face is very handsome. His eyes are inlaid with colored paste. His headband is decorated with silver.

His racing dress is called a *chiton*. It is made as though it were a beautiful Greek column.

Delphi Museum
Photographs, Alinari

Pictures of athletes often decorate Greek pottery. On the right is a painting on a drinking cup, a *kylix*. It shows a tired athlete holding out his kylix for some wine. His oil jug and *strigil* are hanging on the wall. Athletes rubbed their bodies with oil before exercising. Afterwards the strigil was used to scrape off dust and mud.

The first Olympic Games took place in Greece in 776 B.C. They were named after the city of Olympia, where they were held.

In ancient Greece statues were made in honor of wise men, who were called *philosophers. Philosophy* is a Greek word that means "love of learning."

This philosopher, made of bronze, has the wrinkled skin and flabby muscles of an old man. His body is stooped with age. His face shows kindness and understanding.

The most famous Greek philosophers were Socrates, Plato and Aristotle.

The Metropolitan Museum of Art
Rogers Fund, 1910

38

This statue of a young boy is made up of two different original Greek bronzes. The head and body were made in two different periods. The early Romans took the statue from Greece to Italy, where it has been ever since.

It shows a boy looking at the sole of his foot, perhaps to remove a thorn.

Capitoline Museum, Rome
Photograph, Anderson

This unusual figure is a clay drinking cup. The Amazon on horseback is leaning against a cone-shaped cup. The cup is painted with the picture of an Amazon and a Greek in battle. The Amazons were women warriors. They were brave fighters and excellent horsewomen.

Vases shaped like heads were made in terra cotta moulds. They were made in two parts and then attached together with a fluid clay called *slip*. Colored slip was used for vase paintings.

The ancient Greeks used kilns, or ovens, for baking the clay that are like the ones that potters use today. The kilns were very large and made out of firebrick. They were heated by a wood fire. Different kinds of clay were heated to different temperatures in order to bake them. All pottery making today is based on old Greek methods.

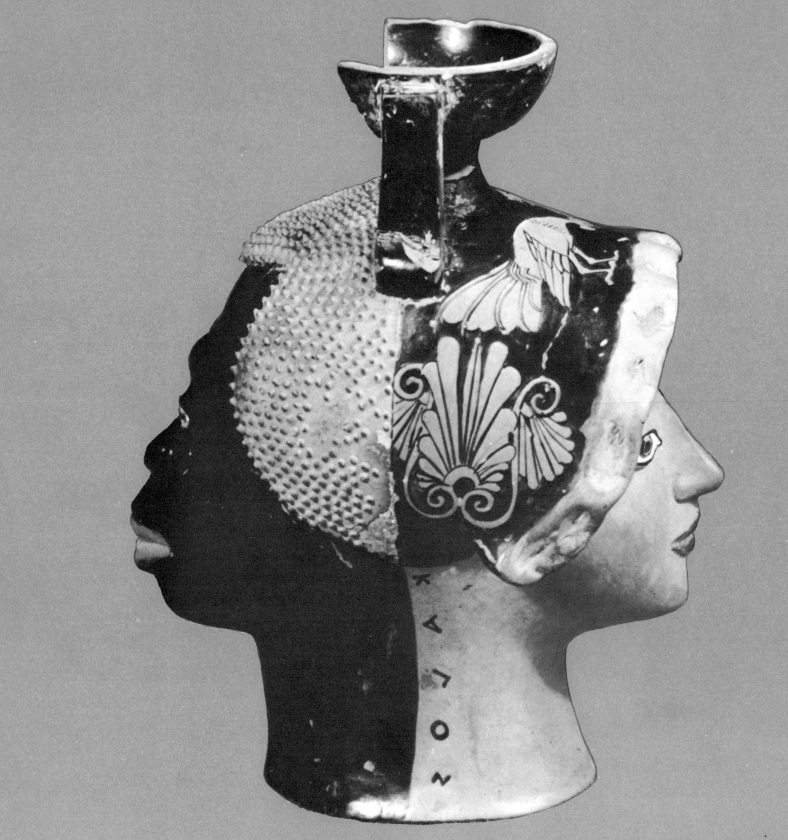

42

reek ships travelled to far-off lands to trade. The Greek artists were interested in the people of these lands. The unusual two-headed vase on the left shows their interest in the people of Africa.

Below is a drinking cup made in the form of a man's head. It has graceful handles.

Most vases for everyday use were not painted.

A little girl with pigeons is the subject of this marble relief. A *relief* is a raised picture against a background.

The girl has a beautiful face. She is like one of the Greek goddesses. She shows great love for the pigeons. She gently hugs one of them, and holds the other with care.

The young girl playing a flute, at the right, is a relief sculpture from the side of an object known as the "Ludovisi Throne." She seems to be listening to the music. One of her legs hangs free to swing to the rhythm of her song.

Her body sinks into the soft cushion. The cushion appears comfortable, even though it is made of stone.

The Metropolitan Museum of Art
Fletcher Fund, 1927

Terme Museum
Photograph, Ali

Archaeological Museum of Istanbul

This is part of a splendid relief which decorated all four sides of a *sarcophagus*, a marble coffin. It is known as "The Alexander Sarcophagus," because the relief shows the adventures of Alexander the Great. Alexander was a king who ruled the Greeks. He was also known as "Alexander the Conqueror." He was very young when he led his armies into Asia and took them as far as India.

Alexander's victory over the Persians is shown on one side of the sarcophagus. This side shows Alexander at peace with the Persians. The Greeks and Persians are hunting lions together. The figures are closely grouped together. They are carved in high relief, which gives them great vigor. The action is lively.

Most sculpture was painted in ancient times, but the paint has worn off. The Alexander Sarcophagus is in excellent condition. Much of the paint is still on the figures. The color makes the figures exciting.

This relief shows a charming figure out of Greek mythology. It is a nymph, a servant of the goddess Persephone. The nymph is putting away bridal linens.

The beauty of Greek art and architecture spread all over the world. It is copied in buildings, sculpture and coins even today. Greek beauty is called "classic."

Their wonderful art brought pleasure to the ancient Greeks, and now, more than two thousand years later, still brings pleasure to us.

From the Frieze of the Parthenon
Courtesy British Museum